Ye have sown much, and bring in little; ye eat, but ye have not enough; ye drink, but ye are not filled with drink; ye clothe you, but there is none warm; and he that earneth wages earneth wages to put it into *a bag with holes.*

—Hag. 1:6

a bag without holes

How to Prepare for
Your Family, Your Finances, Your Future

by

Fred W. Eggerichs

with Bernard Palmer

BETHANY FELLOWSHIP, INC.
Minneapolis, Minnesota

Published by Bethany Fellowship, Inc.
6820 Auto Club Road, Minneapolis, Minnesota 55438

Printed in the United States of America

Library of Congress Cataloging in Publication Data:

Eggerichs, Fred, 1912-
   A bag without holes.

    1. Stewardship, Christian.   I. Title.
BV772.E4   248'.6   74-23435
ISBN 0-87123-532-3

Contents

5

Introduction

I had a lucrative real estate business in southern Florida when the invitation came from a national Christian organization to join their stewardship department. Closing my office and moving north was difficult. Our income would be lowered substantially at a time when we were looking forward to the profits of the next few years to build our savings for the future. Yet one thought kept going through my mind, and eventually it was the deciding factor: Only what you give to God while you are living will you be able to keep for eternity.

Now I can look back on more than twelve years of helping Christians plan their giving to the Lord's work. I realize that I have not only been able to make a contribution to promoting the gospel but have brought deep satisfaction to those whom I have been privileged to serve.

There was a MRS. HENDERSON (not her real name) who told my wife, Esther, and me that she has never ceased thanking God for prompting her to seek help in the area of stewardship.

"You can't imagine how relieved I am to know that my financial affairs are in order," she said. "I'll be taken care of until the Lord calls me home, my grandson's education is provided for, and the missionary work my husband and I have been supporting since we were married will get a gift that should help them continue after I'm gone."

There was the elderly couple on a farm in Nebraska who had no children. Their closest living relative was an alcoholic nephew who acted as though he didn't even know they were alive except when he wanted to borrow money that he could never remember to return. Had he inherited their estate, as he most certainly would have without a will, their savings of a frugal, hard-working lifetime would have been squandered quickly. And receiving such a sum of money would probably have harmed him; in his condition it could not have helped.

All of that was taken care of, and the bequests to several ministeries would help to present Jesus Christ to many who had never before heard of Him.

"You don't know how good I feel about the way we have worked things out," the husband confided to me. "I've been concerned for some time because Mother has never done much business. Now our financial affairs are set up so she won't have to. If I should go first she'll be taken care of as long as she lives. Nobody can come along and fleece her out of it." His smile broadened. "I can just see the people in the office of that missionary group when they get a letter from our attorney about the money we're leaving them." He leaned forward. "They ought to be able to do quite a lot with $75,000 or $100,000, oughtn't they?"

Then there was the elderly unmarried lady on Social Security who had only her meagre savings. It was not much, compared to the estate of the Nebraska farmer, but her concern in seeing that her holdings were placed wisely after she was gone was as strong and as commendable as theirs. So was her satisfaction.

"I used to worry about it," she told us. "I wanted the Lord to get what little I have. I didn't want it going to the government or some unbelieving relative. Now I know what will happen to my savings."

Those people and most of the others we have helped realized the fundamental truth in the statement about giving to God while they were still living. It is indeed the only way we can keep anything for eternity.

Most men and women have worked hard all their adult lives and have spent wisely in an effort to provide for the future. Some have lived sacrificially in order to give to their Christian interests. Yet many of those same individuals neglect to properly prepare their financial affairs in order to direct the disposition of their assets after their death.

Only a few of those we have assisted would have been able to give very much in cash at the time we visited with them. With limited funds and the uncertainty of the future they felt obligated to keep most of what they had for emergencies. However, the laws of the various states and the provinces of Canada make provision for them to give to the various Christian activities that the Holy Spirit has made precious to them and still provide for their own needs and those of their families.

The circumstances are not the same for everyone. The plan that is ideal for a couple in their seventies would not be practical for their married son with small children to support and educate. A husband with an invalid wife has different needs and responsibilities than the man who isn't married and doesn't plan to be.

For this reason a variety of methods of giving have been worked out over the years: trust agreements, annuities, insurance, joint accounts, outright gifts, and wills. Each has its place and is suitable for given situations. The laws that govern them are complex and differ from state to state. Only an expert in the field can make recommendations with confidence.

That is the purpose of this book. Drawing

upon our training and our years of experience, we will be setting down the various means of deferred giving. Along with listing their advantages and disadvantages in general terms, we will recommend the types of situations each is best suited for.

The advice in this book is not intended to take the place of competent legal counsel. Wills and other legal documents should always be prepared by a respected member of the legal profession. The law hinges on detail and honors only that which is clearly and legally set forth. A misused word or a forgotten phrase can often void a will or contract.

Even if it were possible for a layman to prepare his own documents, the laws differ so widely in the various states that it would be impossible to prepare one volume that would be accurate everywhere. In order to be sure that your wishes are carried out exactly as you want them to be, consult an attorney who works daily within the framework of the laws of your state.

We want to challenge you with the importance of providing for the Lord's business in your estate and to acquaint you with the various means of deferred giving that you can use to accomplish that purpose.

You may wish to seek the counsel of the stewardship department of one of the many Christian organizations that provide such help without charge. Or you may know exactly what you wish to do and can go to your attorney to have your plans carried out. The important thing is that you do it soon while there is still time.

1

Wills

It has been estimated by authorities in the field that 60 to 70 percent of the people in America who die every year do not have *wills*. That statement is not exactly true; everyone has a will whether he makes it legally binding or not.

If you have a legal will drawn up, it will be honored by the court, and your property will be distributed according to your wishes. If you haven't made a will, your state will provide you with one. It won't be called by that name but it will function in the same way. Your property and money will be distributed according to the laws of descent and distribution passed by the legislature of the state in which you live.

State law may be completely contrary to any of your wishes, but it must provide for the distribution of your property if you have neglected to set down your wishes in a legal manner.

In such cases the administrative costs are considerably higher and the administrator is fenced in by the rigid limitations that the law places on him.

The administrator will have to furnish bond, an expense that can often be saved in the case where the executor of a will is a trusted member of the family. In addition, any situation outside his narrow powers that might need attention will have to be brought to the court for a ruling. Each court appearance increases the costs.

The LINDGREN family was prominent in the little midwestern community where they lived. The pioneer parents owned a successful dry goods store. They had three children—a daughter who survived them by several years and two unmarried sons. When the parents died the brothers took over the business and operated it until they in turn both died. Their sister had died some fifteen years earlier.

After the death of the last brother, the only living relative of the family, a nephew, discovered that none of the dead family had made a will, and that none of the five estates had been probated. Only one legal course was open to him: He had to first settle the estate of his grandmother, then that of his grandfather, then that of his mother, and finally the estates of his two uncles.

The affair was in the courts for at least five years. Before it was finished every attorney in the small community in which they lived was involved in it. Unraveling the twisted skein created by neglect caused the costs to skyrocket. Much of the considerable holdings the family had acquired had dwindled away. Careful planning could have saved large portions of the legal fees and court costs and several years of delay in obtaining legal possession of the estates.

The difficult situation of the Lindgren nephew, however, is not the only type of problem that is caused by those who neglect to make out a will. In some states the law stipulates that a widow without children will get half of her husband's estate. The rest will go to the husband's parents or next of kin—a brother, sister, or any close relative. Many widows have been stunned to learn that their husband's neglect in making out a will has cost her half of their modest holdings. Although such a widow may wish to keep her property, it often has to be sold in order to make the division of the estate to satisfy the law. She will have to manage on half of what she and her husband thought she would have.

Others, confident that they would have enough to care for their modest needs, find that the law's division of their husband's estate (when there was no will) has cut into their expected income to the extent that they have had to sell their homes or go on welfare aid. In such cases a will would have transferred the ownership of the estate according to the choice of the husband. His widow would be adequately cared for.

Through a recently developed Uniform Probate Code a group of attorneys and law professors are challenging some of the inequities of the probate system. This is part of an attempt to standardize laws between the various states, an important matter in these days of family mobility.

The Uniform Probate Code assumes that a man would make out a will only if he wishes to disinherit someone in the settling of his estate, and that he would normally provide for his immediate family. Written in 1969, it automatically gives the widow the first $50,000 of any estate. The balance would be equally divided among her children.

Only five states have enacted the code or parts of it, but interest is growing and undoubtedly more states will eventually adopt the code in its entirety or in parts. However, it will probably be years before the new procedures gain wide legal acceptance. And even though it should be universally adopted it would not be an adequate legal device for believers who wish to leave anything to the Lord's work because it makes no provision for charitable giving. That purpose must be accomplished by means of a personal will.

Some young couples feel they have so little

that there is no need for them to have a will. They place their car, home and bank account in joint ownership with full rights of survivorship and think that that is sufficient. Even here a will is much wiser for a number of reasons.

Accidents are the principal cause of death among the young, and double indemnity clauses in insurance policies in case of accidental death are common. A young man of modest circumstances can easily leave an estate of $50,000 or $100,000 because of the accident clause in his insurance.

If both the husband and wife should die in the same accident, there would be no provision for the final distribution of their estate without a will. More important, joint ownership does not permit a couple to name the guardian they wish for their children if the lives of the parents are taken at the same time.

A few years ago a young couple who were serving God in the Salvation Army were killed in a car accident, leaving three children under nine years of age. Since there was no will, the court awarded the children to their mother's older brother, the next of kin.

Humanly speaking the choice was excellent. The new parents were quite wealthy and were able to provide for the children very well. The youngsters had every advantage that an affluent home could provide. Moreover, the new parents had only one child, and were willing to legally adopt the three children. This assured the court that the family would be able to stay together and that the children would never become wards of the state.

Yet there was a problem that would have been of vast importance to the deceased parents, although the court would never have considered it. The new mother of the bereaved children was mixed up in an Eastern cult, and her husband was a militant atheist. The children of godly parents were sent into a home where they would never hear the Bible or be guided in prayer. Unless God should intervene, it was not likely that any of the three would embrace the Christ who meant so much to their natural parents.

It would have been so simple for the Salvation Army captain and his wife to have designated a Christian guardian for their children. If the deceased parents would have done this through a will, the court would have been meticulous in seeing the desires of the parents carried out.

In another case an elderly woman turned all her property and savings over to her only son and his wife who had no children, with the unwritten aggreement that they would support her for the rest of her life. They carried out their share of the agreement as long as they lived, but they were both killed in a highway accident.

The wife lived a few hours longer than her husband.

The law is explicit in cases where there is no will and a couple has no children: The heirs of the one who lives the longest, even though it is a matter of minutes, inherits the estate. Since this couple did not have a will, the wife's parents were awarded the estate, and the husband's mother lost the property that would have supported her, forcing her to accept welfare aid.

A will gives the individual the opportunity to allow for emergencies or special conditions. For example, a wife may not be capable of handling large or complex holdings. Some elderly widows have never written a check or made out a tax return before the death of their husbands. Through a will it is possible for a man to name an expert to guide his wife in getting what she needs and in conserving the estate.

A friend of ours who has a number of small children specified in his will instructions for channeling funds to any of his children who might develop special physical difficulties.

"While we love our children equally [we are paraphrasing his will], we recognize that they may not all have the same needs in the future. In the event of the deaths of both my wife and me, the executor of our estate is directed to provide the funds necessary to care for the one (or more) in the unlikely event of

19

serious incapacitating illness or accident. This is to be done even though it may cause an uneven distribution of our property among our children.''

In cases where both younger and older children may be left, a will allows the parents to provide for the care of the minors until they are out of school, until they become of age, before the estate is divided. Because some individuals mature faster than others, parents may feel that the new legal age of eighteen is too young for their son or daughter to handle sizable amounts of money or property with wisdom. It is possible to arrange for his share of the estate to be held in trust until he reaches a designated age.

Exceptions can be made for college expenses or for unexpected physical problems. A will permits the owner of the property to designate exactly how and under what conditions the property is to be distributed.

One wealthy family was faced with the problem of leaving their estate to their son who would never be able to handle wisely the vast amount of money that would be coming to him. Their will provided for the establishing of a spendthrift trust; the income would be parcelled to him every month. In that way they were assured that their grandchildren would also benefit from their estate.

When we first began making stewardship

calls we were surprised to learn that many well-meaning Christians neglected to make wills. Some found it distasteful to think seriously about the time when they would die. Others let the press of family or business push it aside. "We're going to make a will just as soon as we get time," they would tell us.

Many postponed the making of a will because they thought the cost would be so high. "I know we ought to have a will," an elderly retired farmer told us, "but I hate to put all that money out to an attorney right now."

In most cases the cost of drawing up a will is nominal. Attorneys know that when they are asked to write a person's will they are virtually assured of handling the estate later. Usually they have a standard fee that matches that of other attorneys in the same locality. If you are disturbed by the anticipated cost, you can phone your attorney and ask him to quote you his charges. He will be glad to discuss them with you.

A few states recognize an oral will under certain conditions. Like the practice of Israel as recorded in the book of Genesis, the individual tells competent, reliable witnesses what he wants done with his property. (Most states, however, do not consider this type of will valid.)

In some states it is possible for one to make a legal will by writing out his wishes in long hand. (In at least one state [Louisiana] such a will does. not need witnesses if it is entirely in the handwriting of the individual owning the property, dated and signed by him.) In all our stewardship experience we have come across only one such will. It was a masterpiece of brevity. The elderly man who executed it had no children and his Christian brothers did not need financial help from his estate.

"I hereby will everything I have to the——" he wrote. Below that all-inclusive statement he wrote his name and the date.

"I know the above signature is genuine," a neighborhood friend had penned an inch below Joe's signature, "because I saw him sign it." A notary public witnessed both signatures.

In the state where this will was made the signatures of two witnesses are required, although it is not necessary to have the signatures on a will notarized. The judge accepted the notary public as the second witness, validating the will.

In this particular situation the legal heirs were thrilled that the money was going into the Lord's work. They had means of their own and would undoubtedly have carried out his wishes even though the court had refused to accept the will. However, it would have been much better to have an attorney see that it was prepared more professionally. It could very easily have been declared void.

In Nebraska a will was made out for a man who was in the hospital for a serious operation. The will was drawn up by an attorney and was given to a son to take to the hospital to obtain the signature of the sick man. Nurses were brought in to witness the signature. However, the patient pushed a curtain between himself and one of the witnessing nurses in an effort to get it out of the way so he could use the flat surface of the night stand to lay the will on when he signed his name. One nurse actually saw the signing of the document, but the other did not. The will was contested and thrown out on that almost ridiculous technicality.

A will that is partly handwritten and partly typed is not legal, but a will that is written both in pencil and pen is valid. Some states do not require witnesses to a handwritten will. Other states make no distinction between handwritten and typed wills. Some states ask for two witnesses, and others require three. If the person making the will holds property in a state requiring three signatures, his will must display the three signatures to be legal and binding there.

These examples are but a sampling of the maze of conflicting limitations and requirements on the making of legal wills across America. With the laws so different in the various states and so explicit in their demands, it is not practical to try to save a few dollars by getting along without a will or to write one yourself. Such economy could well cause a person's holdings to be distributed far different from his wishes.

It is important to know that the dower or homestead rights of a widow cannot be taken away by a will. Nebraska and Tennessee, among other states, require that at least one-third of a man's real and personal property must go to his spouse when they have children. If there are no children she is to receive one half.

In most states a will is necessary to channel property from one who has died to the surviving spouse in order to qualify for the maximum marital deduction from inheritance taxes. The late United States Senator ROBERT KERR made a will when his holdings were valued at $50,000, and was in the process of making a new will when he suddenly died.

The old will, almost hopelessly obsolete, was probated. Since it did not take advantage of the marital deduction, the entire estate was taxed. His holdings were valued at $20,800,000, but the final probating expenses and federal and state taxes depleted more than half of it. The family had to borrow $6,000,000 to pay the federal estate tax. If the new will had been completed, it would have saved many thousands of dollars of the estate.

Five states declare a will to be void if a child

is born after the will is made. Other states have laws guaranteeing children born after a will has been signed will receive the same share of the inheritance as the other children.

Some states require that certain relatives be' specifically named (under certain conditions) in the will in order to show that they were not forgotten. However, in one will filed for probate in Kansas, the will stated, "And for my nephew, John, that no good rotter—not one red cent." John sued the estate for slander and was awarded more than he would have obtained if the will had included him in an equal distribution of the inheritance.

In some states a will must be in effect for a certain period of time before it is regarded as valid. In California Mrs. Brown added a codicil to her will, leaving her estate to two Christian organizations just twenty-eight days before she died. Her nephews and nieces challenged the will because of a clause in the law that stated a testator had to live for thirty days after writing a new will in order for it to be valid. A compromise was agreed to out of court, awarding the relatives a third of the estate and each of the Christian groups a third.

If the following statement had been added to the codicil, all of the estate would have gone to the Christian organizations, since such clauses have been ruled legal in the courts of California: "If for any reason my will should

be contested. I will my entire estate to Mr. D——
L——. Mr. D—— L—— could be the president
of one of the organizations, and he in turn could
have divided the estate as the original owner
wanted it done. However, an inheritance tax
would have had to be paid under this arrange-
ment.

To increase the complexity of the laws governing wills and estates, some states insist on
fixing a limit on the percentage of an estate
that would be permitted to go to a charitable
organization in cases where close heirs are left.
Those percentages vary from state to state.

MR. AND MRS. ADAMS lived in a small
town in western Iowa but did most of their
trading in Nebraska. Out of habit they went to
an attorney on the west side of the Missouri Riv-
er to have their will drawn up. They wanted
half of their estate to go their children and the
other half to a certain charitable organization.

Their attorney prepared the will exactly as
they asked him to without checking the laws of
Iowa, assuming that they were the same as those
of Nebraska. Some time later he confided in a
close friend, who happened to know that in their
particular situation, Iowa laws allowed only a
maximum of 25 percent to go to charity. They
took the faulty will back to their attorney who
made the necessary changes.

Choose the executor of your estate wisely.

He will be placed in charge of all of your funds and property and will be supervising your real estate, investments and other assets during the period of administration of your estate. He will be reviewing the value of your securities and real estate for the purpose of selling those that are the least desirable in case cash is needed. He will be preparing and filing the required income tax returns and will be paying all the necessary state and federal taxes.

If you do not have complete confidence in the integrity and business perception of a close relative, approach a qualified friend who is younger than you are, or seek the services of one of the officers in the bank where you do business. The delegation of such authority is too important to parcel out to an unqualified person, regardless of his relationship to you.

Although everyone should make a will, there may be better ways to provide for the distribution of your estate for the Lord's work. Revocable and irrevocable gifts, annuities, life estate agreements, savings accounts, life insurance and many other methods are available. We will discuss them in detail in subsequent chapters.

If you have made out a will, it should be updated if there have been any changes in the circumstances of your life since your will was drawn up.

REASONS FOR UPDATING YOUR WILL

1. If you have married.
2. If a child has been born.
3. If you have moved to another state.
4. If your income has changed greatly.
5. If you have purchased additional property, either in your own state or in another state,
6. If you need a testamentary trust placed in your will.
7. If someone among your close heirs has died.
8. If your executor has died, or has been incapacitated by reason of health or age, or has decided not to act for you.
9. If you are in a new business.
10. If your children are no longer minors and you have no need of a guardian for them.
11. If your will has been misplaced or is not in a location where it can easily be found after you have died.
12. If you want to include a Christian organization in your will.

2

Gift Annuities

A *gift annuity agreement* allows a person to make a gift to an organization and still receive an annual income from his investment.

Two elderly women (whom we will call the DAVIS sisters) wrote to a large Christian organization to inquire about *gift annuities*. They were both unmarried school teachers who had been living together since their retirement.

They had been thrifty all their lives, raising a large garden and spending only that which was absolutely necessary. They had never owned a car or taken a vacation more than two hundred miles from home. Although their salaries had never been large, they managed through the years to save a sizable amount which was in an interest-bearing account at their local bank. They both loved Jesus Christ and wanted Him to have the bulk of their savings.

Yet they needed the income while they were alive.

Gift annuities were ideally suited to their situation. The money would be given to the Christian organization at the time they purchased the annuity, and payments from the annuities would be larger than those they were receiving from their bank savings. That was important to them because they were both in their seventies and had no other source of income except their small social security checks.

They were also excited about the fact that they would be making an immediate gift to God's work. The law, which rigorously controls annuities in order to protect the purchaser, permits the charitable organization to take a certain portion of the amount invested for use in their work. The amount is controlled by the age of the purchaser and creates no risk on the part of the purchaser. The balance, which is called the actuarial value, must be invested in sound securities to assure payments to the donors.

In addition to the sum that they were using to purchase annuities, the Davis sisters had additional money available for emergencies such as illness or unexpected repairs on their property. This was important since annuities are irrevocable: once they have been purchased, there can be no refund.

By accepting a little lower rate of return

they were able to have the agreement made out to cover both of them. In that way there would be a guaranteed return as long as one or the other lived. There was also an income and estate tax advantage, but this did not concern them. They were no longer paying any income taxes because of the size of their income, and their estates were not large enough to be affected by estate taxes.

Their first gift annuity was for $1,000, well above the minimum of $500 set by the organization for an agreement covering two or more persons. After a few months they bought another gift annuity, and still later another one. It wasn't long until they had invested a total of $15,000.

"The last time I stopped to see them," related my friend, who is in the stewardship department of the organization that provided them with their gift annuities, "only Edith was at home. Ellen Ruth had fallen and wrenched her hip. She was in a home that could provide bed care for her."

"You don't know what it means to us to have those annuities," Edith volunteered to him. "I don't suppose Ellen Ruth will ever be able to come back here and live. We talked about it a long time the other day before they took her in the ambulance. We just thanked God we had bought those annuities. It means a lot to us to know that the Lord's work is going to get the money we worked so hard for all those years

31

we were teaching." The Davis sisters, now in the twilight of life, were comforted by the knowledge that they were doing what they could for the kingdom of God.

An elderly Christian (whom we will call MRS. THOMPSON) was in an entirely different situation. She was a wealthy widow, and was attracted to annuities by the tax advantages they offered. She had some stocks that had made a considerable gain in value over three or four years (shares she bought for $7,000 were later worth $10,000). She did not want to keep them any longer, but also did not want to pay the capital gains tax on the increase.

The gift annuity she bought was issued for $7,000, so there was no capital gain to her personally. The $3,000 above the original cost of the stock she gave to the organization. Had she taken out a gift annuity for the fair market value of $10,000, there would have been a tax on the long term capital gain of $2,100.

TABLE FOR LONG TERM CAPITAL GAIN ON APPRECIATED PROPERTY
Designed for a Gift Annuity

1. Fair market value $10,000
2. Cost to donor 7,000
3. Actuarial value of gift annuity based on the age of the donor 7,000
4. Percentage of cost to actuarial value (line 3 divided by line 1) 70%

5. Cost allocated to actuarial value
   (line 4 multiplied by line 2) 4,900
6. Amount of long term capital gain
   (line 3 minus line 5) 2,100

She not only avoided paying the capital gains tax, but was allowed a tax deduction of the gift portion for income tax purposes. Had the $3,000 gift put her over the 30 percent limitation on appreciated property for gifts to charity for the current year she could have carried the excess over to succeeding tax years for the next five years.

In addition to the substantial tax gains, Mrs. Thompson received $560 payments each year on her $7,000 annuity, of which only a small part was taxable.

Any appreciated property (like Mrs. Thompson's) can be assigned to any charitable organization that offers annuities. The gift annuity will be issued on the current fair market value of the property and will have the same tax advantages as outlined for Mrs. Thompson.

MR. HARTINGTON had still another reason for wanting a gift annuity: He was in ill health and was concerned that he might die before he could complete the purchase of an annuity in the normal way.

"I'm sending this cashier's check for $10,000," he wrote. "Please buy me an annuity for that amount immediately. The only living heirs I have are my brother's two sons. They're not believers and aren't worthy to get the money my wife and I worked so hard for. I'm going to see that at least this much of my estate will be taken out of their hands and put into the Lord's work."

His fears of early death proved groundless. His gift annuity was processed through regular channels. It was necessary to get his birth date, his social security number, the type of annuity he wanted, and certain other information. He bought the original annuity and later bought two more of similar amounts, and is still drawing checks from them.

On September 19, 1972, the Internal Revenue Service issued new tables which affect the actuarial value, gift portion and exclusion ratio. The new tables enable an annuitant to receive a much larger gift portion than was formerly allowed.

Most Christian organizations have standardized their rates of payment through the Committee on Gift Annuities. However, there are some slight variations in payment rates.

There are four types of gift annuities, designed to meet four specific situations.

Single Life Annuities

The single life gift annuity is the type Mr. Hartington and Mrs. Thompson purchased. It is designed for one individual only. The rate

34

is determined by the person's age. He will be paid that amount as long as he lives.

Joint and Survivorship Annuities

Although *the joint and survivorship gift annuity* is intended for a husband and wife, it can be purchased by any two people, whether or not they are related. It is the plan the Davis sisters selected. The rate is based on the ages of both persons, and is paid to them jointly until one dies, when the payments then automatically go to the survivor for the rest of his life.

Survivorship Annuities

A survivorship gift annuity is the same as the joint and survivorship annuity, except that the payment is made in sequence: It is paid first to one of the holders as long as he lives, then goes to the second individual for the rest of his life.

Deferred Gift Annuities

There is a fourth type of annuity that can be combined with the three just described: the *deferred gift annuity*. It is intended for the person or couple, usually younger than the average purchaser of annuities, having no special need for additional income now but may have later. Payments on this type of annuity do not begin immediately, but are written up to begin when the purchaser wants them to begin—when he reaches a certain age. A deferred gift annuity cannot be altered after the initial purchase.

MR. AND MRS. RUARK were in their late forties. Their children were established in homes of their own and they were at the peak of their earning power. When they made an inquiry about gift annuities, they weren't looking for an immediate return on their investment as their retirement was yet in the future.

We recommended a deferred gift annuity. The Ruarks decided that payments should begin when Mr. Ruark reached the age of sixty-five. The rate of income would be based on their ages at the time the payment would begin. The plan was coupled with the joint and survivorship plan described above, assuring them of an income as long as either one of them lived.

The deferred gift annuity allows a sizable income tax advantage when issued. This pleased the Ruarks very much because they were at the peak of their earning power and could take full advantage of this deduction.

The Ruarks found this to be an excellent way of making a gift to the Christian school that they had attended and also of providing income for their retirement.

Annuities Through a Will

Giving a gift annuity through a will is a form of giving that is recently coming into public acceptance. It is an excellent way of providing for a beloved relative, friend, or even a former employee, and of giving to God's work at the same time. You can designate a certain amount of your estate's assets to be used in purchasing from any Christian organization that issues annuities, an annuity based upon the plan of your choice. The rate will be determined by the age of the beneficiary at the time of your death, and payments will be made as long as he lives.

Some husbands use this method in order to provide for their wives. It spares the widows the responsibility of managing the funds and assures them of a fixed income as long as they live.

GIFT ANNUITIES

Advantages

1. They usually provide a higher return than from savings or other sound investments.

2. There are certain income tax advantages when they are issued, and a portion of the payments are not taxable.

3. Payments are guaranteed for life.

4. There is an immediate gift to the Christian organization, as well as a potential gift if the person dies before the actuarial reserve is exhausted.

5. The cost of the annuity is transferred out of the purchaser's estate. Therefore there is no inheritance or estate tax liability.

6. In the case of deferred gift annuities, payments begin at a future time selected by the purchaser

so that the money will be available when he needs it the most.

Disadvantages

1. They are irrevocable; once an annuity is purchased there can be no refund. For this reason they are not advisable for individuals or couples with limited resources.

2. Deferred gift annuities are not suitable for older persons.

3

Revocable Gift Agreements

A *revocable gift agreement* is a flexible method of providing a gift for an organization while still retaining the earned income during the lifetime of the donor.

MRS. DAVIS, or so we will call her, is one of those kindly, dedicated Christian women who is so concerned about the Lord's work that she could never turn down an appeal for funds. Her husband had handled all their financial matters before his death, and she devoted her entire life to caring for their only daughter, who was both retarded and physically handicapped. When Mrs. Davis needed money she asked her husband for it or used one of their charge accounts. It is doubtful whether or not she had ever written a check.

When her husband died she wrote to a Christian organization that meant much to her, and asked if one of their stewardship representatives could call on her. She had decided she wanted her estate to go to Christian work after her departure from life.

He suggested a revocable gift agreement. It was likely that she would outlive her daughter, but she had no assurance that she would. "We have to think of her welfare first," he said. "You should not do anything that might deprive her of proper care. Your assets should be available to you or the executor of your estate in case your daughter outlives you."

Her husband had been a successful businessman and had left her a sizable amount of cash, stocks, and twenty-five residential lots in a subdivision that was not quite ready for development. Mrs. Davis saw that a revocable gift agreement was the best type for her because she could add to it or take away from it as her needs or the needs of her daughter changed. She would be giving to the Lord's work and yet would be safeguarding herself and her daughter.

That was in 1962. Her daughter died a few years later at the age of twenty-five. Today Mrs. Davis is living in Sweden so that she can be near her sisters.

"You don't know how wonderful it is for me to know that a Christian organization is taking care of my investments," she told a friend shortly before going to Sweden. "They were such a worry to me when I was trying to handle them myself. Now I get the checks from my earnings every month. I have plenty to live on and I know that three Christian groups are going to share in my estate when I'm gone."

A close friend of hers wrote to the Christian organization, "I just have to tell you how thankful those of us who love Mrs. Davis are that you have that agreement with her and are handling her property. I'm sure she would have given away every cent she had years ago if she hadn't placed her property in your hands."

A man whom we will call MR. DONNELLY was faced with a different problem. He was well able to handle his financial affairs while he lived, but was concerned about the care of his crippled daughter after his decease. She was confined to a wheelchair and was unable to care for herself. The chances were that she would never marry or be able to earn her own living. He had to be sure that there was enough money available to take care of her.

He turned several thousand dollars worth of stock over to the stewardship department of his denomination in a revocable gift agreement. After his death the dividends were to be paid to his daughter (or her guardian) as long as she lived. The agreement was revocable only to Mr. Donnelly and would become irrevocable at his death.

God continued to bless him in his profession

and he added a savings account and two pieces of property to the agreement within the next few years. The flexibility of such an agreement makes it possible to add or subtract property or revoke it entirely. Dissolving the contract is simple, requiring only the signing of a revocation form and (in the case of real estate only) the drawing of "quit claim" deed.

When Donnelly's daughter died two years after he went to be with the Lord, their denomination was able to cash in the stocks, close out the savings account and sell the real estate immediately. The proceeds were available for any pressing need; there was no waiting for probate and there was no possibility that the courts would nullify the agreement. It showed the true intent of the donor and was not subject to review.

Some types of agreements are only profitable for the organization that has them if they are in sizable amounts. However, this is not true with revocable gift agreements. An agreement of any size can be used profitably.

MABEL PETERSON wanted her Christian witness to go beyond her daily contacts to distant shores. She was concerned about those who had never heard of Jesus—particularly those in Indonesia and the Philippines. She read all the literature that came to her from those two countries, and corresponded with a number of missionaries.

She wanted desperately to help in a financial way, but had not yet found a convenient way to do it. She had worked in a supermarket most of her adult life, standing behind a check-out counter day after day. Her income was barely above her living expenses and tithe, and only spartan discipline gave her any savings at all. Still, she wanted her savings to go into missionary work after her death.

She first wrote to a large faith mission and apologetically asked if they would be interested in the gift she was able to give. "I can only manage one hundred dollars in cash right now," she explained, "but I might be able to add to it from time to time."

With her best interests in mind they set up a revocable gift agreement, thinking she might have need for her small savings at some time in the future. But they did not reckon on her tenacity or devotion, for she kept increasing the amount in the agreement until it was more than five hundred dollars. Then she inherited a small house from an uncle and added it to the agreement.

She is still at the check-out counter and is still saving. Once or twice a year they receive a small check from her to add to the total amount. She knows she can cancel the agreement or withdraw the money or the property from it at any time, but only a staggering financial problem would cause her to do so.

43

Mabel Peterson's present situation seems to be the same as that of the majority of those who make revocable gift agreements. Only a fraction of such gifts are ever recalled, according to the testimony of the Christian organizations that I have contacted. The records of one large charitable organization reveal that more than 96 percent of their revocable gift agreements are left in force until the death of the donor.

Under certain restrictions the organization may use the money deposited with them if that privilege is stated in their contract. They must first get a signed statement from the donor, giving his permission for its use at a specified rate of interest (or at no interest at all, providing that fact is clearly stated). They must have the money available on demand, either in cash or in sufficient collateral so they can get a bank loan to repay it if the donor asks for its return.

This is done most often by schools for dormitories, scholarships or student loans. Other groups may do it for capital improvements, such as erecting new buildings or buying needed equipment. The procedure is a means of providing capital at a lower rate of interest than that charged by banks.

Many Christians are thankful for the opportunity to have a part in helping to solve the immediate financial needs of one of their favorite Christian organizations by permitting the money in their revocable gift agreement to be used for a limited time in this way with their full knowledge and consent.

Discretionary Revocable Trusts

Banks and savings and loan associations have a simple way that an individual can transfer his savings account to the Lord's work at his death: the discretionary revocable trust. The agreement is so simple that some financial organizations have a card printed especially for that purpose, and those who have savings deposited with them have only to fill out the card naming the trustee and the beneficiary, then dating and signing it. When the card is given to the bank, the agreement is immediately in force.

The donor actually names himself the trustee while he is living. In that capacity he is able to add to the account or withdraw money at any time. No one else can make withdrawals or deposits or change the conditions of the account in any way. As long as the donor lives he is in complete control of the account, even to the extent of closing it or rescinding the agreement if he wishes.

A successor trustee (a younger person is preferable) becomes active only at the donor's death. When he presents the original donor's death certificate to the savings institution, the account is transferred to the beneficiary—in this case a Christian organization. There are no delays, closing expenses or probate. The entire amount of the account is transferred immediately to the particular Christian group that the donor has indicated on the card.

Not all banks and savings and loan associations, however, are aware of this type of trust. A couple whom we will call Dr. and Mrs. Terrill discovered this when they were making plans for a trip to the Near East. A few months before they left, they had inherited a sizable sum of money which they deposited in a savings account in their bank. The balance of their estate was properly set up, but nothing had been done about the new savings account which they wanted to go to a certain Christian organization. They were concerned about what would happen to the account if an accident took their lives.

Hearing of a discretionary revocable trust, Dr. Terrill went to the bank and asked for a card to sign in order to place the account in such a trust. The officer eyed him blankly.

"Why don't you make it a joint account, using the name of the organization as the second party?" he suggested.

Dr. Terrill didn't want to do that. "I'm sure they wouldn't make withdrawals unless something happened to my wife and me, but they could. I don't believe it's good business to set it up in such a way that this would be possible."

"Then I'm afraid we won't be able to help

you," the banker replied. "We don't offer a —what did you call it—a discretionary revocable trust?"

"I'm sorry to hear that. I know the bank up the street has that service."

"They do?" Doubt edged his voice.

"I've seen the printed cards they use. If you can't take care of it I'll move the account over there."

The officer excused himself for a hurried consultation with the bank president, who made a telephone call. "We have just talked with our attorney who is drawing up a—a discretionary revocable trust agreement," the officer offered. "If you'll stop back the day after tomorrow, you and your wife can sign it."

This is now a service this bank offers to others who, like Dr. Terrill, want their savings or checking account to go into the Lord's work.

REVOCABLE GIFT AGREEMENTS

Advantages

1. The donor can designate the beneficiary, and still retain the income from his gift for his lifetime.

2. He can cancel the agreement at any time.

3. He can avoid the cost and delays of probate on the amount of the gift.

4. He can be sure his gift will not be nullified by disgruntled heirs breaking his will.

5. He can add to the agreement or take away from it easily at any time.

47

6. He can designate that the returns be paid to someone else.

7. He does not have to have a large amount of money or a piece of property available before starting the program. In most cases as little as $100 is sufficient.

Disadvantages

1. He has to pay income tax on the returns from the property or cash until such time as it is irrevocably given to the charitable organization.

2. The organization cannot use the money or property until the death of the donor unless written permission is granted.

4

Life Estate Agreements

A *life estate agreement* is a method of transferring real estate to an organization while still retaining full control of the property during the lifetime of the donor.

JOHN and MARY SMITH had an attractive three-bedroom home in a prosperous Minnesota community of 15,000-20,000. Two years earlier their only son had taken over the family business when John retired because of ill health. They were planning to retire in Florida and were thinking about selling their home. The value of the property had sky-rocketed, however, and they realized that they would have to pay a capital gains tax of several thousand dollars.

It was then that Mary suggested giving the house to a Christian organization that meant almost as much to them as their local church. John had no objection; in fact he was enthusiastic about the idea. But he was a cautious man. He didn't know how well they would like living in Florida and felt that it was unwise to do anything that couldn't be undone.

"If we only knew we were going to like the country and the people around Fort Myers, it would be different," he said. "But we might hate the place. Or there might be some financial reverses at the store, or one of us might get sick. If any of those things happened, we would need the money that the house would bring."

Investigation proved that the stewardship department of the Christian organization that they were interested in had a financial plan that was devised for donors in situations such as theirs: a revocable life estate agreement. The agreement would permit them to deed their home to the organization, effective at their death. They could live in their home or rent it out and receive the income from it. And they could cancel the agreement and reclaim the property any time they wished.

Since the gift was revocable, they would have to pay the taxes and the upkeep on the property, and be fully responsible for its management. For obvious reasons, few organizations will pay for the taxes, expenses, and management of property given in a revocable life estate agreement.

The only tax advantages to the Smiths would be the avoidance of the capital gains tax and the inheritance and estate taxes. To gain an income tax deduction the gift must be irrevocable. But they decided to sign the revocable agreement.

After Mary's death some nine years later John made the agreement irrevocable. "That house meant a lot to her," he explained. "Giving it to the Lord was her idea. I won't be revoking it now."

HARRY ELLIS had felt called to Africa as a missionary when he was in Bible school, but ill health kept him home. He was always interested in the people of a certain central African country and wanted to do what he could to help the faith mission that was working there.

He had not done extremely well financially but had managed to buy two houses that gave him a rental income in the little Kansas town, in addition to the one he and his wife lived in. They wanted to do something for God, and at first considered selling the homes and giving the money to the mission.

He was hesitant to dispose of the property, however. A recurrence of the heart condition that kept him from the field as a young man might force his retirement. If that happened they might need the money those two homes would bring.

After consulting with the stewardship department of the mission, he deeded the houses to them in a revocable life estate agreement.

The agreement gave him the right to take back the property at any time during his lifetime or that of his wife.

A revocable life estate agreement is versatile in that it permits a variety of options to meet differing conditions. The donors could have given the rental money to the mission or to anyone else they named. They could have named two or more charitable organizations to share their gift. The original agreement was made with one organization, while the others, if included in the agreement, would have received their share of the gift at the donor's death. The only stipulation is that the recipients of such gifts must be registered with the United States Internal Revenue Service and have a tax-exempt status.

Harry and his wife had the joy of giving while still alive, without the risk of not having the money available to meet some unexpected emergency such as illness or financial reverses. Yet they received the income that their gift produced just as though they held the deed themselves. They had to pay income tax on the rent money they received. They also had to pay the taxes and upkeep on the property. The government takes the position that since holders of revocable agreements receive the income from their property, and at the same time retain the right to reclaim their property, they still own the property. It would become a gift only at the donor's death.

Not long ago I made a call on a woman who was very concerned about her home and what would happen to it when she died. She had no living relatives and was afraid the house would be left standing empty for months while the estate was dragged through the courts in probate.

"I want my home and the antiques I've collected to go into the Lord's work," she said. "Is there some way you can arrange it so someone will take charge of it right away and dispose of it?"

I informed her there was. A life estate agreement seemed most suitable. She needed the house as long as she lived and wanted it to go into the Lord's work promptly upon her death.

She was greatly relieved. "A friend of mine passed away a year or so ago," she said. "She didn't have any relatives either, and her home was left empty. You should have seen what the vandals did to it! They broke out half the windows and carried off her prettiest and most valuable things. Half of the rest of them they broke up or damaged."

"We would have someone here in a matter of a few days," I assured her. "He would supervise the disposing of the property and see that everything was taken care of just the way you would want them to be."

A life estate agreement is actually a contract between the donor and the organization. The donor turns the property over to the organization with the privilege of taking it back at a later date. The organization, in turn, agrees to pay him the income earned from the property during his lifetime. The income from the property may also be paid to anyone else the donor wishes to name.

ANNA, an elderly widow in one of our western states, insisted on making an *irrevocable* life estate agreement from the beginning. The stewardship representative who covered the area where she lived was apprehensive when her letter came in, outlining what she wanted to do. He knew she possessed little more then her home and a $2,000 annuity that she also insisted on buying.

He counselled with the men in the office and decided to call on her when he was in her area. Sitting in her living room a month later he explained that giving the property irrevocably could cause problems for her. "You might have an extended illness that would make it necessary for you to raise all the money you can," he said. "You already have the annuity and that cannot be given back to you. Part of it has gone into the ministry and the rest has been invested to provide you an income. I would strongly advise you to reconsider and give your home on a revocable agreement. Then you could get it back in case of some unforeseen development."

"That's exactly what I don't want to be able to do," she retorted, eyes flashing. "I'm in my right mind now and I know what I want to do. I was born in this house and I expect to die here. I want God to have my home. If I get sick or need care, I know He will take care of me." With some reluctance the organization wrote up the contract, which she eagerly signed.

Irrevocable life estate agreements were not developed for such individuals as Anna. We would not recommend that anyone else follow her example. Still, we have heard the same desire expressed by many others during our years of experience in helping people give to their favorite charitable organization.

The irrevocable life estate agreement is for the person who is sure he will not need his property again and wants to obtain the maximum tax advantage. In such cases the Christian organization usually sells the property and invests the proceeds. The earnings are then returned to the donor.

In the case of the elderly widow who died soon after she deeded her property to the Christian organization, circumstances worked out according to her faith in the Lord. The Christian organization was notified there were some unpaid expenses after her funeral, and when the home was sold the remaining bills were paid out of the proceeds. Surely the Lord supplied.

55

LIFE ESTATE AGREEMENTS

Advantages

1. The donor retains control of the property during his lifetime.

2. Estate settlement costs are reduced.

3. Immediate distribution is made upon the death of the donor.

4. The agreement may be revoked at any time. (This would not be true, of course, if an irrevocable agreement was drawn.)

Disadvantages

1. There are no immediate income tax savings, except in the case of an irrevocable gift.

2. The donor maintains the property and pays all taxes, insurance, etc., except in the case of an irrevocable gift.

Revocable and Irrevocable Mortgages

PETER NORRIS and his wife wanted their son to have their home after they moved to a warmer climate to retire, but they needed additional income for their own living expenses. They had an interest-bearing *mortgage* on the home drawn up for their son. After the son paid on the mortgage for a year, the Norrises gave the mortgage to a Christian organization irrevocably. (They could have made it a revocable gift agreement if they had wished.)

The payments on the mortgage went to the Norrises as long as they lived. Upon their deaths the mortgage payments would go to the Christian organization.

A gift of this type is highly variable. The mortgage was originally for $21,000. The Christian organization could have received a sum very close to that amount, or they may have gotten only $6,000 to $8,000. Since both of the donors were in their seventies and the payments were substantial, it was entirely possible that they would get even less than $6,000. It could have been possible that the son would have paid off the entire amount before they both died. Nevertheless, this is a good way of giving to the Lord's work.

Had the Norrises been content with a 6 percent return on the mortgage, the Christian organization could have set up a life income annuity trust (see chapter 5), a plan with two advantages for them. First, they would have gotten an income tax deduction based on their ages and the rate of return. (It would have been deductible on the donor's income tax return the year the agreement was signed, and would have amounted to a sum up to 30 percent because the mortgage was on appreciated property. They still would have had the privilege of the five-year tax carryover on the balance.) Second, not all of the return would have been ordinary income as some would have been considered long-term capital gain.

It is not feasible to transfer mortgaged property into an annuity trust because of the capital gains tax chargeable to the donor. It would be

considered more of a bargain sale agreement
(see chapter 9). However, the Norrises were
giving a mortgage and not their mortgaged property.

5

Life Income Agreements

A *life income agreement* is still another way of giving real or personal property when the donor wants to gain the maximum tax advantage and still receive an income from it. It must be given irrevocably in order for the Internal Revenue Service to count it as a deductible item.

In most cases property given in this way has greatly appreciated in value during the time it has been in the donor's possession. If he were to sell it, the capital gains tax would be staggering.

This was the situation MARTIN RUSSEL found himself in. Just prior to World War II he bought a forty-acre parcel of land about a mile from his home in a city in the South. Everybody claimed that the real estate agent took advantage of him because of his youth and inexperience, pawning the apparent worthless patch of grubby forest off on him. A little ravine scarred the only open land in the entire forty acres, and many considered the property so poor that he was foolish even to pay taxes on it.

Then industrialization hit the city and it exploded in all directions, sprawling out over the neighboring hills. Martin's land, scarcely worth holding for the more than two decades he had paid taxes on it, was eagerly sought for building sites. He was offered a staggering price for it, but the capital gains tax would have depleated so much that he hesitated to sell.

Instead, he deeded it to a Christian organization with the stipulation that he would be given $2,000 a year until his death or to the end of a ten-year period, whichever came first. Martin felt he needed an additional $2,000 income. He could have set the figure at $3,000 or more per year if the recipient had been agreeable, or he could have made it $500, or $1,000. In an agreement of this kind the exact terms can be worked out between the donor and the recipient organization.

In this case the Christian organization was able to work out long-term leases for at least six parcels of business-zoned land and was in the process of negotiating with other buyers. The organization could have sold the land outright in parcels, and paid Martin a stipulated return each year on the money they received from it.

Martin's income from the agreement was taxable, but he did not have to pay the capital gains tax on the increased value of the land since he did not receive it. Moreover, the fair market value of the property, computed by a treasury department table based on the amount of return he received and his life expectancy, was figured as a contribution, deductible up to 30 percent of his adjusted gross income (he could carry the balance over for the next five years). This represented a substantial tax saving for him.

There are three types of life income agreements: the annuity trust, the uni-trust and the pooled income fund. Although they all possess the same general characteristics, each is designed for specific situations and purposes.

Life Income Annuity Trusts

The *annuity trust* is much the same as an annuity. The income tax benefits come the year the agreement is signed and the gift is irrevocable. When stocks or real estate has been given in any annuity trust, it is gone and cannot be returned to the previous owner. Furthermore, when an agreement is made it cannot be changed. If Martin, for example, had decided to give another piece of property, he would have had to enter into a new agreement regarding it.

Although it is possible to set up an annuity

trust agreement with any agreed size of yearly, quarterly or monthly payments (the latter in the case of large amounts only), the rates are usually based on a fixed percentage not less than 5 percent. (This is not true in the case of the pooled income fund agreement where the payments are made on the money actually earned by the property.) Unlike an annuity, however, the recipient of the gift cannot use any of it until after the donor's death.

Not long ago we visited with a widow who wanted to deed her home in a life income agreement. In discussing her financial situation we discovered that she had only the house and a small bank account. The slightest emergency would have created a hardship for her.

We suggested a revocable gift agreement if she were determined to make a gift. While she was considering the matter, a routine medical checkup revealed that she had a malignancy and needed cobalt therapy. We were thankful we had counselled her as we did. If a gift is not wise for the donor to give, neither is it a wise gift for the organization to receive.

LIFE INCOME ANNUITY TRUSTS

Advantages

1. There is an income tax advantage the year the gift is made. Under certain conditions this can be spread out over five years in order to take advantage of the 30 percent allowance for the contributions per-

mitted by the Internal Revenue Service. If the gift is in cash, a 50 percent allowance is given.

2. There is an avoidance of the capital gains tax which goes up to 25 percent in the case of very large amounts.

3. The principal becomes the property of the charitable organization immediately upon the death of the donor or income beneficiary.

4. There is no further management responsibility for the donor.

Disadvantages

1. The gift cannot be used for the Lord's work until the death of the donor or the income beneficiary.

2. Once the agreement is signed it cannot be changed or cancelled.

3. It is impractical for those with limited funds.

Life Income Uni-trusts

Essentially the *uni-trust* is the same as an annuity trust. It is an individual trust set up in the same way—an irrevocable gift agreement. It can be a cash deposit or real estate or other property of value. Once it is signed it cannot be altered.

There are differences, however. The law requires that the assets of a trust be valued each year and that the interest payment be at a fixed percentage, but it must be 5 percent or more. A number of charitable organizations we are familiar with pay 6 percent as a guaranteed payment. Payments in a uni-trust must be paid according to one of three plans. The desired plan must be chosen at the time of the purchase.

(1) Plan One guarantees that the purchaser will receive the agreed percentage each year, even though the principal may be somewhat depleted to make the required payment.

MISS BARBER, a spinster living on the West Coast, inherited $10,000 in stocks from her father. She placed them in a uni-trust with a Christian faith mission operating in Indo-China. The agreed annual payment was to be 6 percent. A year after she made the gift, the stocks soared to double the par value and there was a stock split, making them worth $20,000. The Mission gave her $1,200, or 6 percent of $20,000. The following year the company was plagued by increasing costs and a crippling strike. The stocks dropped to $16,000 in value. This time her 6 percent payment was $960.

The rate of interest remained the same, but the amount of her payments fluctuated. If the stocks had not earned enough to pay the 6 percent agreed upon, the difference would have been drawn from the principal.

(2) Plan Two is different from Plan One in that any deficiency in paying the agreed percentage payment will be made up the following year, if possible, or any succeeding year.

If Miss Barber's choice had been Plan Two, her stocks would have earned only 5 percent the second year. She would have received only that percentage (as under Plan One). But if on the third year they would have earned 8 percent, she would have earned the agreed 6 percent *plus* an extra one percent to make up the deficiency of the previous year. If the stocks had earned 10 percent on the third year, she would still only receive the agreed 6 percent.

(3) Plan Three is different from the other two plans in that there is no provision for the makeup of prior deficiencies.

If Miss Barber had adopted this plan, she would have received 5 percent on the second year and 6 percent the third, in spite of the fact that the earnings the third year were much higher than the agreed 6 percent.

LIFE INCOME UNI-TRUSTS

Advantages

1. In regard to taxes, they are the same as that for an annuity trust.

2. The principal becomes the property of the charitable organization immediately on the death of the donor or the income beneficiary.

3. There is no management responsibility for the donor.

4. The minimum percentage of income paid to the donor is fixed by law.

5. Plan One guarantees the agreed percentage.

6. Plan Two provides for deficiencies in the earnings to be made up in subsequent years. (Plan Three is the same as Plan Two except that deficiencies in earnings are not made up.)

Disadvantages

1. The gift cannot be used in the ministry of the Christian organization until the death of the donor or the income beneficiary.

2. Once the agreement is signed it cannot be changed or cancelled.

3. The agreement is impractical for those with limited funds.

4. The agreement is also usually considered impractical for those wishing to make gifts of less than $10,000. (Some Christian organizations will not write a uni-trust for less than that figure because of administration difficulties and other problems relating to reinvesting the principal.)

Pooled Income Funds

The *pooled income fund* agreement is intended for the person who prefers the features of the uni-trust agreement but does not want to give that large a sum.

That was the position CLARENCE BUDD found himself in. He had $5,000 he wanted to give to a certain Christian organization in a uni-trust agreement, but they did not accept a gift that small. The stewardship executive who counselled with him suggested a pooled income fund agreement.

In most of its essential details it is the same as a uni-trust, he was told. "The gift is pooled with other gifts in the same category for the purpose of the investment; the basis for figuring the returns on the gift to the donor is different;

and the agreement is open-ended. It can be added to at any time," the stewardship representative informed him. "We only ask that the additions be for a thousand dollars or more." Clarence liked the provisions of this type of agreement and readily made his investment in this way.

Each donor is credited with one unit for every $10 that he gives. If he is credited with 500 units and each unit earned 6 percent, his return for the year would be $300. If each unit earned 5 percent, his checks would total $250.

These payments would be made semi-annually until the death of the donor or the income beneficiary. There is no guarantee of a specified return as there is in payment Plan One of the uni-trust agreement. Neither is there a guarantee of a fixed percentage with losses made up in subsequent years as in payment Plan Two. The donor in a pooled income fund agreement receives the interest actually earned by the fund, regardless of how great or how small the return is.

POOLED INCOME FUNDS

Advantages

1. The advantages are the same as those in a uni-trust except that there is no guarantee of a fixed return on the gift. Payment is made according to the percentage of return the fund has earned. All of the income is disbursed to the donors.

2. Smaller amounts may be given.

3. Additions can be made to the agreement without legal complications.

Disadvantages

1. The gift cannot be used in the ministry of the Christian organization until the death of the donor or the income beneficiary.

2. Once the agreement is signed it cannot be cancelled.

3. There is no guarantee of a specified income from the investment.

6

Short Term Charitable Trusts

TED McCORMICK'S construction company was booming. He had launched a large housing project in a Milwaukee suburb at a time when the construction of homes lagged behind the demand for them. The homes were being sold as fast as his crews could complete them. Although he was not sure the trend would last beyond his current project, it had lasted long enough to give him large profits which put him in an uncomfortably high tax bracket.

He was a Christian and realized that the time had come to increase his giving. In going over his financial status he saw that for at least ten years he would not need the income from the $30,000 in stocks he owned; so he placed them in a *short term charitable trust* with the Christian college that his two daughters were attending.

The trust was set up for ten years. At the end of that period he must decide whether to cancel the agreement and have the stocks returned to him, or leave them with the school until he needed them later or until he reached retirement age. The income of approximately $1,500 a year would go directly to the school during the period they held the securities. McCormick did not have to pay taxes on them or even report them. And, because the stocks were in a trust of this type, he was able to contribute the interest on the stocks in addition to giving the normal 50 percent tax deductible portion of his annual income.

The contractor did much better financially during the next ten years than he had anticipated. His income did not take the drop he expected when the housing project was finished, and he was able to leave the securities in trust until he reached retirement age. At that time he gave it to the school in a life income agreement, with the returns to be paid to himself and his wife. Then the stocks would become the property of the school when they died.

Short term charitable trusts are not limited to stocks and bonds. They can be used to channel the returns from any income-producing property into the Lord's work for a limited period of time. Such trusts are not written to be in effect for less than ten years.

Obviously this type of giving is not wise for

every person in every type of situation. It should be used by those who don't need the income from a particular piece of property (either real or personal), but do not feel they are in the financial position that would make it possible for them to make a permanent disposal of either the income or the property. If you are in that situation, the short term charitable trust may be exactly the type of agreement that would best fit your needs.

SHORT TERM CHARITABLE TRUSTS

Advantages

1. A short term charitable trust provides immediate income for the charitable organization.

2. It permits the donor to reclaim the property on a specified date (not less than ten years but at any time later).

3. It provides a legal means of giving beyond the 50 percent limitation for charitable gifts that the Internal Revenue Service permits with income tax credit.

Disadvantages

1. The property cannot be reclaimed for the duration of the agreement.

2. Not all charities are elegible beneficiaries. (If you are considering a trust of this type, check with the Christian organization that you wish to make the agreement with to see if they qualify.)

71

7

Year-End Gifts

In southern California another contractor was going over his income on the day after Christmas. He, too, had earned more that year than in any previous year. At the end of the year he would find himself in a much higher tax bracket. He was a dedicated believer with a concern for his church and for the organizations spreading the gospel on high school and college campuses. He decided that it was time for him to review his giving.

He and his wife first considered a short term charitable trust; but, since he was planning to expand his business within the next few years, he thought he might need the property as security for a loan.

Outright gifts seemed to be more practical for them in their financial situation. He got out the appeal letters that had come the previous month, and he and his wife went over them carefully. They would be able to give more at this time with less cost to themselves than at any time since they were married. They wrote out a sizable check to the mission fund in their church and to two other organizations that seemed to have a greater need at the moment.

Actually, year-end giving is practical for anyone whose income fluctuates from year to year. A farmer who gets along with less hired help, or a small businessman whose wife takes over as bookkeeper and clerk, may find himself in a higher tax bracket at the end of the year because his deductible expenses are lower, making his profits proportionately higher. Farmers often find it advantageous to give an extra gift at the end of the year. So may salesmen, business and professional people, and those with investments in stocks and bonds and real estate.

MARTIN found himself approaching the end of a certain year in a higher tax bracket. He is a free lance writer who does a great deal of travelling for research, a deductible expense. But this particular year a big project kept him home at his typewriter for several months, when ordinarily he would have spent three or four thousand dollars travelling. His income remained substantially the same, but he realized that the drop in travel expenses would have the same effect as an increase in royalties. Year-end giving proved to be a good thing for him and his wife.

ARTHUR hadn't planned on selling the cattle he was feeding until some time early in January. This had been his policy for years. However, corn was in short supply, the price was good and gave no indication of going higher, and his steers were far enough along to make an earlier selling of the cattle practical. There was an income tax problem, however, since the sale of the cattle would increase his profits by several thousand dollars.

He, too, decided that the end of the year would be the best time for him to make the contribution he had been thinking about. He wanted to give enough money to his denomination's mission hospital in Zaire to air-condition the operating room. It was not until the afternoon of December 31 that he made the decision, however. Since he lived sixteen miles in the country, he phoned his attorney to see if a check could be made out that day and mailed the next time he came to town.

"It will have to be in the post office today in order for you to get credit on this year's income tax," he was told. "It doesn't have to be in the office of the recipient, but it does have to be in the post office early enough to be postmarked."

Arthur had a sixteen-mile drive over icy roads to get his check in to the post office before it closed. He made the trip in time to fulfill the rigid Internal Revenue Service requirement for year-end giving.

YEAR-END GIFTS

Advantages

1. The donor can decide when giving is most advantageous to him personally, such as a year when his income has been high or his deductible expenses lower than normal.

2. He does not make any commitment for the future and has full control of his property at all times.

3. His gift is available to the Christian organization immediately.

Disadvantages

1. All income has to be reported and the gift deducted as a contribution. This may cause the donor to be placed in a higher tax bracket than if some other form of giving had been used.

2. The gift becomes a part of his total contributions allowed by the Internal Revenue Service (limited to 50 percent of the donor's gross income with certain restrictions).

3. The Christian organization has no assurance that the gift will be repeated a second or third year, which makes it difficult for them when making plans to expand their work.

8

Life Insurance

HENRY ROBERTSON had been forced to leave high school when he was in the eleventh grade because of the death of his father. He started to work in the local dairy to help support his mother and two sisters. He did so well on his new job that the dairy gave him a permanent route within a few years. He was able to provide a comfortable living for his own family. However, the job was not the kind that would accumulate a sizable estate for him.

He loved the Lord, and was particularly concerned about the ministry of the Christian radio broadcast that he listened to every day as he made his rounds. He and his wife sent in small contributions from time to time, but they often wished that they could do something more substantial to help the ministry.

There was little chance for them to save any

more than they were saving, and they had no stocks or real estate to give. They couldn't even buy a deferred annuity.

"I know what I can do!" Henry told his wife excitedly one evening. "I can take out an insurance policy on my life and make the broadcast the beneficiary. That way they would get a gift when the Lord takes me home."

When he wrote to see if the organization could be named as the beneficiary on an insurance policy, he discovered that it was a regular feature of their stewardship program. He also learned that the premiums he paid would be deductible as charitable gifts.

"All you have to do to get the income tax benefits is to have the policy written in such a way that the beneficiary is a charitable organization," he was informed. "You can retain the right to change the beneficiary if you desire. In fact, there is an additional tax advantage in retaining control of the policy to this extent. [We will explain the circumstances in which that is true later.] But if you want to deduct the premiums as a contribution, the policy has to go to one charitable organization or another."

This is exactly what the Robertsons decided to do. The income tax deduction was helpful to him. Because they were comparatively young they bought a policy that would mature in twenty-five years. At maturity or at Harry's death the insurance would go to the gospel broadcast

77

that meant so much to him. He could have purchased a simple life policy and have had a larger amount for the program, but that would have
meant that the Christian organization would
have had to wait until his death to benefit from
it.

Friends of the Robertsons wanted to help
their denomination by contributing to a revolv-
ing fund to assist struggling churches. The husband felt their insurance program was inade-
quate. His wife was named the first beneficiary
on his policies, but they had no children and
had made no provision for a second beneficiary
if they were both killed in the same accident.
He added the name of their denomination as the
second beneficiary. In that way he was taking
care of his obligation to his wife and seeing
that the Lord's work would get the amount of
the insurance policy in the event they both died
or were killed.

He could have set up the policy in another
way: naming their denomination the sole beneficiary, with the provision that an annuity be
set up to make certain payments to his wife
from the life insurance proceeds until her death
or until the account was depleted. Any balance
in the account would be transferred automatically to the denomination at the death of the
wife.

Since life insurance dividends are not taxable

as income, either the Robertsons or their friends could give those dividends to the Christian organization and take credit on them as contributions for income tax purposes. Or they could use the dividends to buy additional insurance for the institution in which case they would also be deductible. Both the Robertsons and their friends chose the latter method.

There would have been even more tax benefits to either family if they had assigned an older policy to the Christian organization. If the Robertsons, for example, had given a $10,000 policy which had a cash surrender value of $5,000, they could have received a $5,000 deduction on their income tax return as a contribution. This tax benefit would be in addition to the other benefit of deducting the annual premiums.

Had the Robertsons' holdings been quite large, retaining 5 percent control of the insurance policy by reserving the right to change the charitable beneficiary could effect sizable savings for his estate. Reserving the right to change the beneficiary would prove ownership of the policy, according to federal law. The policy could then be added to his estate to increase his net worth, thereby providing a larger figure to divide through the marital deduction, which is one half of the estate. Then the entire amount of the policy could be deducted from the estate as a charitable contribution.

LIFE INSURANCE

Advantages to the Donor

1. Life insurance provides a way for those with limited income to give sizable gifts.

2. It provides immediate income tax benefits.

3. Under certain conditions it provides additional estate and inheritance tax benefits.

Advantages to the Christian Organization

1. Money is provided immediately on the death of the donor without delays or the expense of probate.

2. The insurance policy becomes a growing asset as the cash value increases. The organization may borrow on the policy at a favorable, guaranteed rate of interest.

3. The organization can look forward to future expansion, knowing this amount of money will be available at the donor's death.

Disadvantages

1. The policy must be irrevocable in order to affect income tax benefits. The beneficiary, if changed, must be another charitable organization.

2. Nothing more than the loan value of the policy is available to the organization until the death of the donor.

9

Bargain Sale Agreements

A *bargain sale agreement* is just what the name implies: Appreciated property is sold by the donor to a charitable organization for less than the property's present fair market value. Such a sale obviously helps the recipient and has certain tax advantages for the donor, in addition to having the satisfaction of contributing to a Christian organization that means much to him.

MR. LEONARD bought a block of stock for $12,000 several years ago, then sold it to a faith mission for the same amount, even though it had increased in value until it was worth $60,000. He immediately received a gift deduction of $48,000 from his income tax return for the year the contract was made. He deducted up to 30 percent of his adjusted gross income that year, and carried over the balance for the next five years. However, Mr. Leonard had to report $9,600 as capital gain, based on government tables.

FORMULA FOR
LONG TERM CAPITAL GAINS

1. Fair market value $60,000
2. Cost to donor 12,000
3. Return to donor .12,000
4. Percentage of cost to sale
(line 3 divided by line 1) 20%
5. Basis allocated to sale
(line 4 multiplied by line 2) 2,400
6. Capital gain (line 3 minus line 5) 9,600
7. Capital gain allocated
to gift portion (not taxed) 38,400

If Mr. Leonard had made an outright gift of his stock, he would have received a $60,000 income tax deduction with no tax whatsoever on the capital gain.

10

Taxes Involving Charitable Gifts

Taxes can play an important part in our Christian giving—such an important part that we should examine our motives as we give.

Why do I want to give? Is it because I am in full accord with the ministry of a certain organization? Do I have faith in the men who will be spending the money? Do I believe that they will allocate it wisely? Am I giving because I love God and want to serve Him?

Giving is an act of worship and should be a result of our devotion to our Savior. God will not honor the gift that is given for any other reason than because the donor loves and wants to worship Him. Any tax credits or other benefits must be secondary in the mind of the donor. We must consider this seriously as we think about the tax advantages that come from certain types of giving.

GIFT ANNUITIES

1. Gift annuities offer a deductible gift on federal income tax returns.

2. The annual payments are largely tax free.

3. The gift portion is not taxed under the federal estate tax.

4. The gift portion is not taxed under the federal gift tax.

5. Gift annuities reduce the tax on capital gains.

LIFE INCOME AGREEMENTS

1. There is an income tax deduction for the amount of the agreement.

2. There is no tax on the capital gains.

3. The gift amount is not taxed at death under the federal estate tax.

4. The gift amount is not taxed as a gift under the federal gift tax.

LIFE INSURANCE

1. Premiums are deductible gifts when the charitable organization is the irrevocable beneficiary.

2. The paid up value of an older policy is deductible when it is given.

3. Dividends are not reported income, and when they are given to a Christian organization they are deductible.

4. The replacement value of a paid up policy is deductible.

Appendix

GENERAL INFORMATION ON TAXES

Federal Estate Tax

The *federal estate tax* is imposed upon the transfer of the decedent's property to his beneficiaries. (Some *states* also levy an estate tax on the property of the decedent.)

1. Gifts to qualified charities are exempt with no limitations.

2. A $60,000 exemption is allowed.

3. An estate may be revalued within six months.

4. If an estate is worth more than $60,000, the executor or administrator must file a preliminary form 704.

5. The final form 706 must be filed within nine months after the death of the owner and the paying of the tax.

6. The marital deduction is allowed under certain conditions. This deduction is 50 percent of the estate.

7. Any agreements where a charitable organization is to receive the remaining interest is also deductible.

The gross estate is valued at the date of death. However, if the executor so elects, valuation is as of six months after the date of death, but if the property is transferred during the first six months, such property is valued as of the date of the transfer.

Federal Estate Tax Rates

Based on net estate before deducting $60,000 exemption.

Net Estate Before Deducting Exemption	Federal Estate Tax	Estate Tax Rate Next Bracket
$ 60,000	Exempt	3.0%
65,000	$ 150	7.0
70,000	500	11.0
80,000	1,600	14.0
90,000	3,000	18.0
100,000	4,800	21.2
110,000	6,920	24.2
120,000	9,340	27.2
150,000	17,500	26.4
160,000	20,140	28.4
200,000	31,500	27.6
300,000	59,100	26.8
310,000	61,780	28.8
500,000	116,500	28.0
560,000	133,300	31.0
700,000	176,700	30.2
810,000	209,920	32.2
900,000	238,900	31.4
1,060,000	289,140	33.4
1,100,000	302,500	32.6
1,310,000	370,960	35.6
1,560,000	459,960	38.6
1,600,000	475,400	37.8
2,060,000	649,280	41.8
2,100,000	666,000	41.0
2,560,000	854,600	45.0
2,600,000	872,600	44.2
3,060,000	1,075,920	47.2
3,100,000	1,094,800	46.4
3,560,000	1,308,240	49.4
3,600,000	1,328,000	48.6
4,060,000	1,551,560	52.6
4,100,000	1,572,600	51.8
5,060,000	2,069,880	55.8
5,100,000	2,092,200	55.0

6,060,000	2,620,200	58.0
6,100,000	2,643,400	57.2
7,060,000	3,192,520	60.2
7,100,000	3,216,600	59.4
8,060,000	3,786,840	62.4
8,100,000	3,811,800	61.6
9,100,000	4,427,800	60.8
10,060,000	5,011,480	61.8
10,100,000	5,036,200	61.0 on Excess

Rates adjusted for state inheritance tax credit.

Federal Gift Tax

The *federal gift tax* is imposed upon the transfer of property by a gift.

1. The first $3,000 of gifts made to any recipient during any calendar year is excluded.

2. A lifetime exemption of $30,000 is allowed.

3. All gifts made to qualified charitable organizations are excluded.

4. A man and wife owning property can count themselves as separate givers and can therefore legally double their gift.

5. The tax is approximately 75 percent of the federal estate tax.

Federal Gift Tax Rates

Net Gift Before Exemption	Federal Gift Tax	Gift Tax Rate Next Bracket
$ 30,000	Exempt	2¼%
35,000	$ 112.50	5¼
40,000	375.00	8¼
50,000	1,200.00	10½
60,000	2,250.00	13½
70,000	3,600.00	16½
80,000	5,250.00	18¾
90,000	7,125.00	21
130,000	15,525.00	22½
280,000	49,275.00	24
530,000	109,275.00	26¼
780,000	174,900.00	27¾
1,030,000	244,275.00	29¼
1,280,000	317,400.00	31½
1,530,000	396,150.00	33¾

87

2,030,000	564,900.00	36¾
2,530,000	748,650.00	39¾
3,030,000	947,400.00	42
3,530,000	1,157,400.00	44¼
4,030,000	1,378,650.00	47¼
5,030,000	1,851,150.00	50¼
6,030,000	2,353,650.00	52½
7,030,000	2,878,650.00	54¾
8,030,000	3,426,150.00	57
10,030,000	4,566,150.00	57¾

Inheritance Tax

The *state inheritance tax* is levied on heirs receiving benefits from an inheritance.

1. Transfers to a registered charitable organization are exempt from tax in the state where the organization is located, and in any other state that has a reciprocal agreement with their state.

UNIFORM GIFT ANNUITY RATES

Single Life

Adopted by Conference on Gift Annuities, May 2, 1974

Age	Rate	Age	Rate
35 and under	4.0%	60	5.5%
36	4.1%	61	5.6%
37	4.2%	62	5.7%
38	4.2%	63	5.8%
39	4.3%	64	5.9%
40	4.3%	65	6.0%
41	4.3%	66	6.1%
42	4.4%	67	6.2%
43	4.4%	68	6.3%
44	4.4%	69	6.4%
45	4.5%	70	6.6%
46	4.5%	71	6.7%

88

Age	Rate	Age	Rate
47	4.6%	72	6.9%
48	4.6%	73	7.0%
49	4.7%	74	7.2%
50	4.7%	75	7.4%
51	4.8%	76	7.6%
52	4.9%	77	7.8%
53	4.9%	78	8.0%
54	5.0%	79	8.2%
55	5.1%	80	8.5%
56	5.1%	81	8.8%
57	5.2%	82	9.1%
58	5.3%	83	9.4%
59	5.4%	84	9.7%

Definition of Terms

A

ACTUARIAL RESERVE—invested amount to insure annual payments

ACTUARIAL VALUE—real worth of property

ADMINISTRATOR—court-appointed person to settle an estate

ANNUITIES—income paid yearly or at other regular intervals

ANNUITIES THROUGH A WILL—testamentary request

ANNUITY TRUSTS—annual payments on various invested amounts

APPRECIATED PROPERTY—property that has increased in value

ASSETS—all owned property, both real and personal

B

BARGAIN SALE AGREEMENTS—sale of property below its market value

BENEFICIARY—one entitled to the proceeds of property

BEQUEST—to hand down or give personal property

C

CAPITAL GAINS TAX—tax on the profit of investments

CAPITAL GAIN—profit from increase in value of real estate, stocks, etc.

CAPITAL IMPROVEMENTS—increase in the value of property through improvements

CASH SURRENDER VALUE—paid up value of an insurance policy

CHARITABLE GIVING—gifts made to tax exempt organizations and corporations

CODICIL—supplement to a will

COLLATERAL—property deposited as security on property

D

DECEDENT—a deceased person

DEED—written instrument conveying title of real estate

DEFERRED GIFT ANNUITIES—payments designated to start at a future date

DEFERRED GIFT—a gift payable upon death or at some future date

DEPLETE—to reduce or lessen

DISCRETIONARY—power to act in a contract or trust

DISCRETIONARY REVOCABLE TRUST—written contract setting forth the power to act as a trustee

DIVIDENDS—return of payments from profits of stock or insurance, etc.

DONOR—one who gives or contributes

DOWER RIGHT—right of widow or widower in deceased property

E

ESTATE—one's entire property, both real and personal

ESTATE TAX—federal or state tax on a person's worth at death

EXECUTOR—one who carries out the terms of a will

F

FAIR MARKET VALUE—value of property at current prices

FEDERAL ESTATE TAX—death tax levied by the federal government

FEDERAL GIFT TAX—tax on gifts levied by the federal government

FIXED INCOME—income agreed upon that cannot be changed

91

G

GIFT ANNUITY—contract between a purchaser and a tax-exempt organization whereby the purchaser receives annual returns based on his life expectancy.

GIFTS—tax exempt contributions

GROSS INCOME—actual earnings

GUARDIAN—one who is legally assigned to take care of a minor or of a person physically or mentally incompetent

H

HEIR—one who is entitled to an estate at death

HOMESTEAD RIGHTS—law in many states exempting a homestead from attachment or sale under execution for general debts

I

INCOME TAX—tax on earnings

INHERIT—to obtain as one's portion

INHERITANCE TAX—tax levied on a person receiving property through inheritance

INTEREST—payment for the use of money

INVESTMENT—money or capital invested for income

IN TRUST—property held in confidence for another person

IRREVOCABLE—incapable of being brought back

IRREVOCABLE GIFTS—gifts of capital investments where only the income is returned

IRREVOCABLE LIFE STATE AGREEMENTS—real estate held with no return except the earned income

J

JOINT ACCOUNTS—accounts held in the names of two persons (either one has the power of control)

JOINT AND SURVIVORSHIP GIFT ANNUITIES—annuities held by two or more persons

JOINT OWNERSHIP—property held in the name of two or more persons

L

LAWS OF DESCENT AND DISTRIBUTION—state laws governing distribution of deceased property

LEASE—rental of property

LIFE ESTATE AGREEMENTS—real estate held until the death of the donor

LIFE INCOME AGREEMENTS—income paid to a donor during his lifetime

LONG TERM CAPITAL GAIN—gain on property held over six months

M

MARITAL DEDUCTION—amount allowed because of marriage

MORTGAGES—a contract pledged as security for a piece of property

N

NOTARY PUBLIC—one who is legally authorized to certify contracts

O

ORAL WILL—spoken will witnessed by two or more persons

P

PAR VALUE—market value of stocks, bonds, etc.

PAYMENTS—yield from investments

POOLED INCOME FUNDS—income earned from investments pooled with others

PREMIUMS—payments (as in the case of insurance—amounts paid by the holder on the policy, usually in installments)

PROBATE—legal proof of will

Q

QUIT CLAIM DEED—issued to release ownership of property

R

RATE OF INTEREST—percentage of return on an investment

REAL ESTATE—land, houses

REVOCABLE—recall or rescind

REVOCABLE GIFT AGREEMENT—written agreement whereby the gift may be recalled by the donor

REVOCABLE GIFT—gift may be recalled by the donor

S

SAVINGS ACCOUNT—an account drawing interest from a bank

SECOND BENEFICIARY—one who is entitled to property after death of first beneficiary

SECURITIES—stocks, bonds, etc.

SHORT TERM CHARITABLE TRUSTS—funds held for a duration of time (usually ten years)

SINGLE LIFE GIFT ANNUITY—annuity for only one person

SPENDTHRIFT TRUST—money released sparingly (to keep a prodigal from overspending his inherited funds)

STOCKS—shares of a fund raised for the business of a corporation

STOCK SPLIT—stock that is divided so that two shares are given for each one held

SUCCESSOR TRUSTEE—acts in place of trustee when he is unable to execute his duties

SURVIVORSHIP GIFT ANNUITIES—annuities paid to one until his death, and then paid to his survivor

T

TAXES—(see under the specifically named tax)

TESTAMENTARY—set forth in a will

TESTAMENTARY TRUST—trust set up in a will

TESTATOR—the maker of a will

TRUST—property held in confidence

TRUST AGREEMENTS—written documents giving power for one person to act for another

TRUSTEE—one who holds property for another

U

UNIFORM PROBATE CODE—code set by a group of attorneys

UNI-TRUST—individual trust agreement

V

VALID—legal or real

W

WILL—legal declaration of a person to dispose of his estate or possessions

WITNESSES—those who see the signing of a document

Y

YEAR END GIFTS—gifts made to take advantage of income tax credits